HOW TO

HAVE A VERY
BAD DOG

KNOCK
KNOCK®
VENICE, CALIFORNIA

Created and published by

Knock Knock
1635-B Electric Avenue
Venice, CA 90291
knockknockstuff.com

Illustrated by Bradley R. Hughes

This book is a work of humor meant solely for entertainment purposes. It is not intended to recommend or advise regarding how to
raise or train dogs. The advice contained in this book is intended
as a parody of dog-training books; actually following the advice
contained herein may not be good for dogs or the people around
them. The publisher and anyone associated with the production
of this book do not advocate animal abuse or breaking the law.
In no event will Knock Knock be liable to any reader for any damages, including direct, indirect, incidental, special, consequential,
or punitive damages, arising out of or in connection with the use
of the information contained in this book. So there.

Every reasonable attempt has been made to identify owners of
copyright. Errors or omissions will be corrected in subsequent
editions.

Where specific company, product, and brand names are cited,
copyright and trademarks associated with these names are property of their respective owners.

ISBN: 978-160106576-6
UPC: 825703-50028-8

10 9 8 7 6 5 4 3 2

CONTENTS

THE BEAUTY
OF THE VBD

1 INTRODUCTION

When you stroll down the street, visit friends, or go to the dog park, you spot them immediately: those very, very bad dogs who jump, sniff, ignore commands, bark, and destroy, seemingly with no effort whatsoever from their owners. It's all too easy to write off such disobedience and destruction as good luck. Achieving the highest levels of poor behavior, however, is no accident: it's the result of a multilayered approach to canine psychology that some fortunate people unconsciously adopt.

If you lack this easy affinity for achieving very bad behavior, don't worry. We're going to lead you step by step through all the secrets—collected in one place for the very first time—to having a spectacularly ill-behaved dog. We'll not only teach you specific ways to foster problematic habits in your dog, we'll also share universal dynamics of the canine nature, helping you to understand this special animal's motivational drives.

Canine Quip

"Let's examine the dog mind. Every time you come home, he thinks it's amazing. He can't believe that you've accomplished this again. You walk in the door. The joy of it almost kills him. 'He's back again! It's that guy! It's that guy!'"

—Jerry Seinfeld

Whether you already have a frustratingly well-behaved dog whose habits you would like to break or you have plans to acquire a new pet, this book will walk you through every stage of the implementation of truly atrocious behavior. If you're in the market for a dog, we'll even help you pick out the breed or combination of characteristics that will give you a head start in fostering chaos. Here is just a smattering of the things you'll know after you've read *How to Have a Very Bad Dog*:

- What type of dog owner you are: needy, narcissistic, parental, codependent, or fashion-forward.

- Whether to buy a purebred from a puppy mill or to adopt a mutt that has a head start on poor behavior.

- The seven primary canine drives and which ones motivate your dog.

- The jackpot theory of variable rewards.

- Why you absolutely do not want to housebreak your dog.

- The joys of humping and crotch-sniffing.

- Sure-fire ways to reward neurosis and aggression.

Before we get to these more advanced topics, however, let's start at the beginning. What exactly is the very bad dog?

Defining the Very Bad Dog

Yes, you know it when you see it, but as with any goal, it's vital to have a clear definition. In short, a very bad dog (VBD) causes chaos wherever he goes. Because there are so many manifestations of the VBD, it can be hard to narrow down specific traits and behaviors. Of course, this constitutes no small part of the glory of the VBD—his endless creativity, uniqueness, and ingenuity. Hallmarks of the VBD include barking, whining, pulling on leashes, destructiveness, stealing, escaping from the house and yard, fighting, jumping around, biting, and—above all—willfully ignoring all commands. Once you've successfully begun the VBD journey, groomers, kennels, and veterinarians will begin to create special rules for your pet. Dog walkers may not want to work with him. Dog sitters will call you crying or quit mid-vacation. Disloyal houseguests will refuse to visit, or ask you to pay for their dry cleaning.

Canine Freedom of Choice

The VBD is what every dog should be: a paragon of dogness. So many owners don't allow their dogs' natural characters to shine. When fostered and nurtured appropriately, however, the VBD's instinctual impulses will take over and present you with an extraordinary degree of resourcefulness. Every day you'll wake up and discover something new, and wonder, for example, "How on earth did he get the refrigerator door open?" Your dog's choices will render you speechless. The breadth and depth of his ingenuity will provide constant amusement and astonishment.

Above all, the VBD is a sentient being who cleverly uses the environment around him (whether the yard or a king-sized bed) for his own pleasure. Intuitive creature that he is, the VBD taps into the psychology of the people he lives with and learns to push the buttons that bring him happiness. Cultivating freedom of thought in your dog is the very first step to transforming him into a bona fide VBD—and it's completely incompatible with traditional "obedience training."

Animal Spending

We love our pets, and one of the ways we show that love is through our wallets. In 2012, Americans spent $53 billion on their companion creatures, up from $29.5 billion in 2002. With a VBD, the money saved on obedience training can be put toward repairing any household damage!

"Obedience Training": Poison or Cure?

Dog obedience training is a booming industry. With oppressive marketing tactics, obedience-training advocates have succeeded in creating significant social pressure to train one's dog. For those who have made the VBD choice, obedience training will drastically compromise your progress.

Not only is obedience training counterproductive, it's expensive and wastes precious time that could be better spent enriching your dog-human relationship. It's also important to remember that obedience training isn't about training the *dog*—

it's about training the *owner*. And do you need training? Absolutely not! Well, neither does your dog.

If your dog has already been through the whole
obedience-training rigmarole, however, don't worry.
There is one advantage to obedience training: if you
enforce learned commands inconsistently or not
at all, then your dog is that much further along the
path to VBD-dom (see chapter 5 for further information). Like in life, sometimes we learn rules just
so we can break them.

The Advantages of the VBD

Merely by reading this book, you've already taken a
big step in the right direction, and you clearly have
some inkling as to why the VBD is so desirable.
While the myriad benefits of the VBD can only truly
be understood by living with one, we'd like to
outline a few of the main advantages to affirm that
you've made an excellent choice.

Codependent Relationships
There is nothing in the world like the love of a
dog. Dog owners (aka "canine companions") feel

an unparalleled bond with their pets. In fact, a full 50 percent of married dog owners state that their relationship with their dog is as close as the one with their spouse. Nurturing your dog's VBD behaviors will only strengthen this connection because your life will revolve around his antics, and all your financial, emotional, and physical resources will be funneled toward his happiness. After spending hours chasing him down, and catering to his every need when he whines or looks bored, you'll be rewarded handsomely with his unconditional love.

Finally, there's nothing like a VBD to really sap your wallet. From sky-high vet bills to the cost of replacing damaged property, VBD ownership will require you to spend, but a heightened sense of codependency will result. If you've ever felt unloved, your VBD will change that! A VBD will reward you with the kind of relationship you may never be able to attain with another human being.

Accessories for Your VBD

There's no end to the accessories that will help increase your dog's very bad behavior merely by irritating her:

- **Purses:** A dog who spends lots of time bagged or held in her owner's arms won't learn how to behave properly on the ground. These dogs begin to fear life outside the bag, become incredibly protective of their owners, and often nip when petted.

- **Carrier:** A German company has created a dog garment that fits around a dog's torso with a handle on top for use on dogs too large to fit in purses. What dog wouldn't react to being lifted from the ground like a briefcase?

- **Outfits:** When you dress your dog up like a doll, she will reward you with very cute bad behavior as a result.

- **Fashion accessories:** Your dog will likely eat any canine fashion accessory, which will likely require veterinary treatment. From pearl dog necklaces to fur barrettes and from cute canine shoes (for all four feet!) to pooch sunglasses, your very bad dog can don the latest fashion.

Freedom from Material Things

We live in a consumerist culture that elevates material goods over relationships, spirituality, and love. The pressure is difficult to escape. Fortunately, owning a VBD encourages you to detach from material things, much like Buddhism.

By a bravura show of desensitization, the VBD will rip the Band-Aid off your need to covet expensive

Hall of Fame: Presidential Pooches

If the most powerful men in the world have chosen to cultivate VBDs, why wouldn't you?

- In the early 1900s, Theodore Roosevelt's pit bull, Pete, bit many a White House visitor and even shredded the French ambassador's pants.

- Franklin Delano Roosevelt's Scottish terrier, Meggie, bit a reporter, and his German shepherd, Major, bit a senator.

- In 1967, Lyndon Johnson's mixed-breed, Yuki, lifted his leg in the Oval Office in front of the Shah of Iran.

but meaningless objects. Once your VBD has shredded your upholstery, chewed your Prada shoes, and dismantled the interior of your car, you'll soon realize that life goes on. The amount of time you once spent caring for your objects will now be available for spending with your VBD. True happiness will be yours for the taking.

Love Me, Love My Dog

Do you ever wonder who your real friends are? While we're stuck with our families, we choose our friends and lovers, leaving us vulnerable to mistakes in judgments of character. With a VBD, you never have to doubt whether others love you for *you*, because only those who truly care about you will tolerate your VBD's antics. When you call to cancel plans because you can't leave your overly anxious dog alone, your true friends will understand, and those that don't, well . . . now you know the limited bounds of their love.

If you're single and you own a VBD, you'll quickly know the true intentions of those you date. If after your dog has bitten your boyfriend, chewed up his newspaper, and peed on his shoes, and he *still* wants to date you, you'll never wonder how deeply his feelings run. You will know that this potential partner will stick with you through thick and thin.

Social Skills

If you've ever felt at a loss for words, owning a VBD will change all that. Everyone loves to hear dog stories—the crazier the better. With a VBD, you'll never have to worry about what to discuss at a cocktail party again. Your VBD will furnish you with an abundance of tall tales for social and professional situations when you might otherwise stand awkwardly by the dip. As the life of the party, you'll soon be regaling a host of admirers as you detail the exploits of your dog.

The VBD gives you a credible-sounding excuse to avoid unpleasant or difficult situations. Owning a pet entails responsibility, and your responsibility, as an owner of a VBD, is simply much greater. Whether you avoid travel to a sales conference because Fido has been kicked out of all the local kennels or end a date early because of Bruiser's separation anxiety, after you read this book, you won't be lying. Blame it on your VBD!

> ## Doggy Dictionary: Yappy Hour
>
> Yappy hour is the time at the end of each day to enjoy a cocktail with your VBD.

VBD, Unfettered

Resistance is futile—cultivating a VBD is not about working, it's about ceasing to work. Thus we impart the greatest secret about attaining a VBD: it's *easy*. You won't have to spend hours practicing or attending classes. Follow the simple directions in this book, and you'll have a VBD in half the time it would take to obedience train! And if your dog is already obedience-trained, you'll learn how to undo all that training and encourage your dog to express his natural desires and instincts. Before we dive into the actual steps of nurturing VBD behavior, let's turn to you. By diagnosing what kind of dog owner you are, you'll be able to customize your own individualized VBD approach to suit your personality and lifestyle.

YOUR VBD
PSYCHOLOGY

2 WHAT NEEDS DOES YOUR DOG FULFILL?

Understanding what role a dog plays in your life is the first step in the cultivation of a VBD. A dog has a beautiful ability to intuit human needs and respond to human emotions. To best harness your dog's innate VBD capabilities, you don't want to work against the unconscious signals you are sending her. Additionally, owning a dog should bring you pleasure, suit your lifestyle, and address your individual psychological dynamics.

Your motivations for owning a dog will, of course, have a strong effect on the type of dog you choose.

Whether you purchase a dog that resembles you or one that compensates for what you lack, your canine selection will reflect your self-perceived identity. The hole your dog fills in your life will influence the way you treat her, directly altering her behavior. A dog who is parented will act very differently, for example, than a dog who functions as a therapist. While both have a wealth of poor behaviors simmering beneath the furry surface, the baby substitute may excel at separation anxiety while the therapist will growl at anyone who wants to climb into your bed. By identifying what kind of dog owner you are, you'll discover the behaviors you will most successfully encourage in your VBD. In this chapter, we'll help you determine:

- Whether your dog plays the role of child, fashion accessory, replacement human, house-hold fixture, narcissistic extension of self, compensation for inadequacy, or therapist.

- How you will treat your dog based on her role.

- Which poor behaviors can be nurtured from which types.

Dog as Child

The recent social shift from dog-as-pet to dog-as-child is pervasive. With the increasing delay in childbearing, often well into one's thirties, many individuals bridge the gap between responsibility-free singlehood and devoted parenthood with a dog. Those who never have children continue to relate to their pets as offspring, referring to themselves as "mommy" or "daddy," and chain pet-supply retailers target dog products for "pet parents." In fact, whole industries have been built on this phenomenon, from doggy day care to pet camp to canine psychotherapy.

If you view your dog as a child, you'll spend inordinate amounts of time discussing your darling's social problems, health, and quirky behaviors with colleagues and friends. You'll baby-talk to your little one, make sure your pup is comfortable under her blanket, and worry when she seems a bit down in the snout. You'll have pictures in your wallet or cell phone to show to anyone who's interested (or not). You'll bemoan the fact that her lifespan is so much shorter than yours.

Treating your dog as a surrogate child offers up many opportunities for VBD behavior. Since your dog will be allowed on the furniture and in your bed, you'll create a tantalizing blend of dog-in-charge attitudes with separation-anxiety neuroses. If you're in a relationship, you will direct your affection away from your partner and toward the dog, instilling in the dog a sense of dominance and entitlement. Because children don't need to be walked, it's likely that you'll underexercise your dog but attempt to make up for it with love, creating poor behaviors related to inactivity.

Dog as Fashion Accessory

Admit it—you dress to get as much attention as possible. When you have a VBD in your purse, you will be noticed. After all, a really cute necklace doesn't pee on clothing displays, yap at Starbucks patrons, or nip valets. Every fashionista needs the latest accessories. The newest trend isn't wearing skinny jeans or owning the latest iPhone—it's a teensy-weensy dog, preferably one that matches your outfits. The owner of the dog-as-fashion-accessory is easy to identify: you love to shop,

Doggy Stats

Whether or not they're VBDs, we love our dogs:

- Dogs live in 44.8 million homes in the United States, 40 percent of all households.

- Average annual spending per dog is $1,500.

- 87 percent of pet owners consider their pets family members.

- 37 percent of owners carry pictures of their pets in their wallets.

- 57 percent of owners would choose their pet as their only companion on a desert island.

- 31 percent of owners have taken off work when their pets are sick.

- 79 percent of pets sleep in their owners' beds.

- 20 percent of owners have ended a romantic relationship over a pet.

- 87 percent of owners travel with their dogs.

- 47 percent of owners purchase more than 10 pet gifts a year; 79 percent give their pets holiday and birthday presents.

- 21 percent of dog owners dress their pets.

take at least an hour to choose your outfits, and regularly max out your credit cards. A toy-sized companion is every season's true must-have.

Accessory dogs are prone to similar types of poor behavior as child dogs. Because they spend all their time with their human, they often manifest separation anxiety. They will also exhibit neurotic behaviors rising out of boredom and inactivity. They are gloriously demanding and can become territorial, snapping at strangers who attempt to traverse the purse wall.

Oddly, many fashion-motivated owners will pay no more attention to their pets than they would their shoes. When dogs are treated as inanimate objects, they are inclined to manifest all kinds of fabulous attention-seeking neuroses.

Dog as Household Fixture

Like the dog-as-fashion-accessory, the main purpose of the dog-as-household-fixture is to complete the owners' sense of what home life should be—regardless of available time or space. These are also the individuals who are likely to have 2.4 children because "It's just what you do."

When choosing a dog to match one's home, breed characteristics are secondary to the aesthetic and image needs of the owners. As you will see in chapter 3, some of the best bad behaviors arise when a dog is selected for reasons other than its behavior and activity needs.

Dogs-as-household-fixture tend to have problems stemming from neglect and an inappropriate environment. Whether the dog has high exercise needs but lives in a tiny apartment, or has a strong social drive but is alone all day, you're certain to find multiple poor behaviors to cultivate when a dog suits your interior design and self-image but not your actual lifestyle.

Dog as Replacement Human

Dogs can be the best companions with whom to share emotional challenges. Owners who suffer from anxiety, depression, or neuroses often find that a dog helps them feel better. Adopting a dog as your confidante can result in a host of hyperattachment canine behaviors.

For some, the issue is trust. Many a woman has muttered, "A dog is better than a boyfriend," while men and country songs tend to claim that only dogs will do them no wrong. Certain owners are motivated by great loss, such as the death of a loved one or a difficult breakup. Still others, who aren't good at relating to people, prefer the unconditional, nonverbal love of canines.

Relating to your dog as a substitute person leads you to translate canine behavior to seemingly equivalent human expressions (anthropomorphization), which can produce fantastically poor behavior. In addition, like the dog-as-child and dog-as-fashion-accessory, the dog-as-replacement-human is likely to dominate your household.

Due to the intense bond you've probably fostered with your dog, she's sure to mirror your problems.

The VBD Fixer-Upper

If your VBD isn't exactly the dog you thought she'd be, not to worry—plastic surgery is finally being offered to the underserved canine community, including these procedures:

- Botox injections for inverted eyelashes.

- More attractive drooping for floppy ears.

- Straightening for floppy ears.

- Nose jobs for pugs, bulldogs, and Boston terriers.

- Elimination of unsightly and unhygienic facial or vaginal folds.

- Chin lifts to control drooling.

Dog as Narcissistic Extension of Self

Dogs who resemble their owners are no accident. Some people choose dogs to mirror themselves

The Castration Conspiracy

As the owner of a male dog, everywhere you turn someone will be urging you to have him neutered. They'll tell you that 6 to 8 million animals enter American shelters every year, of which 3 to 4 million are euthanized. But what does that mean for your VBD—and, more to the point, you?

Your VBD won't be able to fulfill his natural instincts to be aggressive, escape your yard, enjoy sex, and spread his seed. You will have to wince every time you think about or discuss "neutering," which is just another word for castration, something you yourself greatly fear. As the owner of a male VBD, you know you won't have to deal with the puppies, anyway.

Most importantly, a neutered dog would not reflect well on your masculinity, something Illinois lawmakers well know. In 2007, the state passed an anti-VBD law that prohibits felons from owning unneutered dogs, claiming that studies show that people with aggressive or vicious dogs tend to have participated in other illegal activities.

If the pro-castration lobby does get to you, there's one last option: Neuticles, testicular implants for dogs. Custom sizing allows you to go as big as you want!

back to them in an endless loop of self-love—
a largely unconscious process. Studies have found
that owners of purebred dogs can easily be
matched by appearance to their pets; this correla-
tion does not exist, however, in mixed-breed dogs,
whose adult appearance could not be predicted at
the time of adoption. This refutes the idea that
pet-owner resemblance occurs over time; instead,
it results from the owner's deliberate choice of dog.

If you choose a dog as an extension of your own
personality, you're likely to have a dog who will
mirror your own behavior. If you're masculine and
aggressive, your dog will be too. Gregarious and
outgoing? Exceptionally beautiful and ditzy? Ditto.
The great thing about this connection is your dog
will also share your flaws, whether or not you
identify them as such.

Dog as Compensation for Inadequacy

Some people choose dogs to represent traits
they themselves do *not* possess. This most often
occurs with men who are insecure about their

masculinity, and they compensate by getting tough, aggressive dogs. If this sounds like you, do not neuter your dog. Who cares about canine overpopulation? You want your dog to display his physical equipment so that everyone will think it represents yours. The more insecure you are, the meaner-looking dog you will get, not to mention that you will cultivate problematic aggressive behaviors to your heart's content so that onlookers will believe you yourself are the tough one.

When women compensate for inadequacy by getting a dog, they frequently find themselves in the show ring with hyperfeminine breeds. Rather than grooming themselves, these women obsessively groom their pet. They believe that if their dog is pretty enough, they'll fly under the radar. These dogs tend to exhibit poor behavior associated with entitlement and boredom.

Your Type, Your Dog

In any pursuit, success is more likely when you go with the grain. Why make things more difficult for yourself when raising a VBD? Choose the dog

Doggy Dictionary: Furkid

If you think of your dog as your child, refer to
your VBD as your "furkid," "furbaby," or "furchild."

and the approach that suit your individual needs.
Of course, when determining which ownership
type best describes you, you may notice that you
fit into more than one category. These types are
tendencies that prove useful in determining one's
pet psychology. The point of this section is utility,
so if you share characteristics of both the dog-as-
fashion-accessory and dog-as-child, by all means,
avail yourself of both sets of poor behaviors!

If you already have a dog, you've no doubt already
instilled some wonderfully bad behavior in your
pet. And if you don't have one yet, the next chapter
will help you determine which dog is right for you.
As many of these types suggest, the most important
factor in selecting a potential VBD is making sure
your decision is based on nothing whatsoever
having to do with the dog. Sound complicated?
Read on and it will all become clear.

THE RIGHT VBD
CHOICE FOR YOU

PICKING OUT
YOUR DOG

It's hard to go wrong when choosing a dog for poor behavior, since dogs are the most diverse species on the planet, with more breed varieties than any other animal. So if you made your choice of dog before committing to the VBD way of life, don't worry, because in subsequent chapters we'll discuss ways to maximize any dog's antics. If you do adopt your pet with the cultivation of poor behavior in mind, you can select for traits and tendencies that will make your job significantly easier.

For those who prefer less work, there is an intuitive way to adopt a dog with a high likelihood for creating chaos. As mentioned in chapter 2, if you

VBD Naming Protocols

	Male	Female
1	Max	Maggie
2	Jake	Bear
3	Buddy	Molly
4	Bear	Shadow
5	Bailey	Lady
6	Shadow	Sadie
7	Sam	Lucky
8	Lucky	Lucy
9	Rocky	Daisy
10	Buster	Brandy

When you choose a name for your VBD, you could choose a fancy American Kennel Club (AKC) name, such as "Champion Gold Mine Diamond Precious Tam o' Shanter," which your dog will never learn. Or pick from among the most popular monikers. When you go to a busy park and call your dog, any number of dogs will become confused and ill-behaved!

choose your dog based on his appearance and whether he reflects well on you, you'll generally wind up with excellent misbehavior. For this, don't read up on the dog's breed, don't worry about where he comes from, and don't question whether he fits your lifestyle. Just get him because he's cute, manly, or whatever else floats your boat.

To go about the selection process more deliberately—whether you're getting your first, second, or even third dog—you'll want to absorb the intricacies of breed, source, and behavioral tendencies.

In this chapter, you'll learn:

- How to match your home environment and your new pet.

- Whether you want a purebred, a designer mixed breed, or a mutt.

- Where to acquire your dog: pet stores and puppy mills versus animal shelters.

- Why you should get more than one dog.

Choosing the Best Dog for Your Home

When adopting a dog, you'll want to consider both your physical home environment and your household's lifestyle. If you live in a one-bedroom apartment without a yard, for example, opt for a dog with high exercise needs so you can focus his energy on a host of destructive tendencies. A herding dog, such as a border collie, requires lots of mental stimulation, so this is the perfect match for someone who's rarely at home. While you're out, your border collie will have plenty of time to explore your personal possessions. A dog, such as a terrier, bred for hunting small game, will shine in a household full of cats. When considering buying a dog for children, take size into consideration. A large, overwhelmingly strong breed, such as a rottweiler, Doberman, or chow chow, will undoubtedly dominate youngsters.

Selecting Dog Characteristics

No matter what breeding route you take (breeder, pet store, or animal shelter), there are a few traits to look out for when selecting your dog. Before choosing, watch the dogs as they interact with other dogs and with humans, and try to find one with some or all of the following characteristics:

- Sensitive to being touched or handled

- Cringes in response to human contact

- Extremely high level of activity

- Aggressive to other dogs; bullying

- Incessant barking or yapping

- Pacing

- Cowering in the corner

- Obsessive paw licking

In addition to observable activity, when you talk to the people from whom you are adopting, keep your ears open for dogs that are described as "protective." If a dog has been in multiple homes, you can practically bet on a wide range of poor behaviors. Finally, a dog with a "Caution" sign on his kennel is always a great choice. By keeping your eyes open and your intuition keen, you'll no doubt spot the seeds of poor behavior to start your journey.

Purebred, Hybrid, or Mutt?

It is said that there's no such thing as a bad dog, only a bad owner. When it comes to the VBD, we make a subtle modification: there's no such thing as a well-behaved dog, only a bad owner. Thinking in this way will prove liberating as you agonize over which pet to adopt. It's true that selecting for certain characteristics will simplify the process of instilling VBD behaviors, but if you are deliberate in your approach, you will be able to turn any good dog bad. That said, there are some tendencies to consider when choosing your adoption approach.

- **Purebreds:** You can bank on known tendencies arising from centuries of breeding for particular purposes. If you really want to excel with a VBD, purebreds are the safest choice, especially if you go with an unreputable breeder, pet store, or puppy mill.

- **Hybrids:** Hybrids are deliberately mated purebreds, an increasingly popular trend of late. For example, the Labrador retriever plus the poodle creates the labradoodle, originally combined to create hypoallergenic guide dogs, while the puggle (pug plus beagle) is just plain cute. While the blending is intended to bring out the desired traits of each breed, fortunately for the VBD lover, this plan often backfires. Weimardoodles, for example, can often exhibit the neurotic and clingy traits of the Weimaraner along with the intelligence and stubbornness of the poodle. When choosing a mixed-breed VBD, be sure to research the character traits of each of the purebred ingredients in order to maximize the potential for poor behavior.

- **Mutts:** When you adopt a dog whose lineage you know nothing about, you're flying blind with respect to very bad behavior. For all you know, your new pet could turn out to be the most mellow, obedient dog of all time. However, if you have a mutt already or believe in rescuing an unwanted animal, with the help of this book, you'll be able to nurture frenzy and lack of control in any dog. You can increase your VBD odds by adopting with an eye toward certain characteristics, however, as outlined in the rest of this chapter.

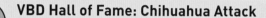

VBD Hall of Fame: Chihuahua Attack

In 2005, a pack of angry Chihuahuas attacked a police officer in Fremont, California. After escorting a teenager home from a traffic stop, the officer was charged by five Chihuahuas at the boy's front door. The dedicated public servant sustained multiple bites to his ankles and was treated at a local hospital.

The Purebred VBD

When choosing the breed for your new VBD, there's no shortage of expertise to rely upon. With many years of selective breeding and behavior observation, you can be relatively certain to adopt a dog with the advertised traits. It's especially important to buy purebreds from pet stores or industrial breeders, as outlined in this chapter.

Hybrids: Worst of Both

Designer mixed breeds are the hottest new trend. The American Canine Hybrid Club, established in 1969, lists almost 450 crosses ranging from the

The Most Popular Breeds—
How Do They Stack Up for VBD?

Breed	Rating	VBD Characteristics
Border collie	🐾🐾🐾🐾🐾	Prone to all sorts of neurotic behavior when living in homes without sheep. Intelligence leads to unparalleled invention of never-before-seen bad behaviors.
Chihuahua	🐾🐾🐾🐾🐾	Extremely prone to aggression. Can be antisocial and high-strung. Frequent yippish barking.
Jack Russell terrier	🐾🐾🐾🐾🐾	High prey and dominance drives. High activity level. Frequently obnoxious. Requires little work to create a VBD.
Weimaraner	🐾🐾🐾🐾🐾	Extremely neurotic: separation anxiety, destructiveness, obsessive tendencies, and overall anxiety. High activity level.
Boxer	🐾🐾🐾🐾	High prey and defensive drives due to former police-dog role. Quick to develop neurotic behaviors like separation anxiety.
Cocker spaniel	🐾🐾🐾🐾	Due to 1950s popularity, often inbred and prone to snappy, domi-nance-related aggression problems combined with timidity, known as "shy-sharp." Puppy-mill dogs prone to wide array of neuroses.

Breed	Rating	VBD Characteristics
Yorkshire terrier (Yorkie)	🐾🐾🐾🐾	Bossy, yappy, stubborn, and notorious for lack of housebreaking skill.
Beagle	🐾🐾🐾	Generally placid and docile. Can be encouraged to howl. Strong pack drive can lead to separation anxiety. Wanderlust. Puppy-mill breeding produces snappiness.
Doberman pinscher	🐾🐾🐾	High prey, high arousal, and high defense drives, but intelligence and intuition mean that hard work is required to produce a Doberman VBD.
Golden retriever	🐾🐾🐾	With high food and social drives, can produce good VBDs as long as not accidentally encouraged to behave. Particularly adept at pulling on leashes and leaping on strangers.
German shepherd	🐾🐾	Well-bred specimens make for poor VBDs, so avoid unless from poor breeding stock, which will result in high defensiveness and aggression fueled by intelligence.
Labrador retriever	🐾🐾	Sadly, most popular dog in the United States. Bred to be submissive and well-behaved. Choose from hunting rather than show lines due to greater energy and higher arousal levels.

affenpoo (*affen*pinscher + *poo*dle) to the zuchon (shih t*zu* + bi*chon* frise). The *-oodle* mixes in particular offer up endless genetically predisposed VBD possibilities. Here are a couple to consider:

- **Chiranian**: *Chi*huahua + Pome*ranian*. A fantastic choice for the VBD aficionado, this dog retains all the desirable VBD traits of the Chihuahua (aggressiveness) and throws in the belligerence and dominance of the Pomeranian.

- **Borderstaffy**: *Border* collie + *Staff*ordshire terrier. What could be better than a pit bull who's really, really smart?

Puppy Mills and Pet Stores: Your Best Resources

Pet stores almost always have highly suitable candidates for a VBD because these puppies are almost always purchased in bulk from puppy mills—breeding facilities in which care and socialization with humans are kept to an absolute minimum during the most important imprinting phase of development, at five to six weeks of age.

Additionally, since puppy mills are fantastically lax about their breeding protocol, the likelihood of recessive genes that can contribute to very bad behavior is increased.

Try to patronize pet stores that avoid questions about where they buy their puppies. Or you can bypass pet stores entirely. Puppy mills now advertise online and will ship your dog directly to you.

Above all, avoid breeders who seem knowledgeable about and caring toward their dogs, especially those who interrogate you extensively about what kind of home you will provide. Instead, go with the breeder who wants to make a quick buck.

Animal Shelters and Rescues

The VBD seeker has to be especially careful when it comes to humane societies and the like, as one can easily wind up adopting a well-behaved, mellow dog. The only reason for a VBD lover to visit an animal shelter is in the hopes of rescuing a dog who already exhibits characteristics of poor behavior, anxieties, or phobias. Try in particular for young, active dogs from one to three years old. These dogs have often landed in the shelters because they exhibited a host of behavior problems after outgrowing their cute puppy qualities.

> ## Canine Quip
>
> *"Dachshunds are ideal dogs for small children, as they are already stretched and pulled to such a length that the child cannot do much harm one way or the other."*
>
> **—Robert Benchley**

One advantage to adopting an older dog is knowing little to nothing about its upbringing. Dogs who have been in rescue for a long time often develop unique behaviors that would be nearly impossible to instill without considerable investment.

Multiple-Dog Households

If you already own one dog, consider getting another, because double-dogging can be a great shortcut to bad behavior. Two dogs in a household

Truth in Advertising

When deciding which dog to choose from an animal shelter, learn the secret meanings behind the words on the dog's information card.

What It Says	What It Means
"Great guard dog."	Aggressive toward anyone who enters your house, whether friend or foe.
"Shy with strangers."	Poorly socialized—will bite or growl at new people.
"Needs an owner who's home a lot."	Cannot be left alone or he will destroy everything in sight.
"Wants to be an only dog."	Will eat other pets.
"Likes to be in charge."	Tendency to control its owner with aggression.
"Needs experienced owner."	Multiple poor behaviors pre-instilled!
"Shepherd mix."	Pit bull.
"Staffordshire terrier."	Pit bull.
"Amstaff."	Pit bull.

will play off each other's tendencies, so that a dog who isn't a barker, for example, will soon learn to mimic his housemate. A dog who constantly has accidents in the house will soon teach his buddy that this is acceptable (and, in fact, preferable), while a dog that has phobias will often transfer his neuroses. You'll get two VBDs without your having to lift a treat. And, if either dog has a propensity for dominance, soon enough they'll both dominate you, and your house will truly be run by VBDs. Three or four dogs are even better!

Let the VBD Begin!

Congratulations on your choice! Remember—even if your dog doesn't fit any of the characteristics or breeds outlined in this chapter, this book will show you how to transform him into a VBD. In order to nurture your dog, you first need to understand him. Canine behavior (as primal, instinctual drives) reaches back into history before domestication. Once you understand these motivations (outlined in the next chapter) and determine which exist in your dog, you can move toward actual VBD activities.

UNDERSTANDING
YOUR VBD'S
DRIVES

WHAT DO THEY REALLY WANT?

While the malleability of dog behavior is one of the features that makes them so appealing, and they are capable of learning many of the lessons we teach them, our beloved animals come to us hard-wired for various tendencies and instincts. These basic, inborn characteristics are called "drives"— some arising from years of selective breeding, a few common to all dogs in varying degrees, and others merely the luck of the genetic draw. In the course of cultivating your VBD, you may be able to modify the expression of your dog's drives, but the drives will never go away. Rather than fighting these drives, you want to harness them to foster poor behavior that goes with your dog's individual character. Just as you learned in chapter 2 to identify your own dog-owning type, so now will you determine your dog's inherent inclinations and then choose behaviors that naturally complement your dog's personality. In so doing you will fully maximize the opportunities for success and make the process fun and rewarding for both you and your VBD. In this chapter, we'll demonstrate:

- What your dog *really* wants from you.

- Why your dog jumps on strangers.

- How to distinguish between the hunt drive and the prey drive.

- What bad behaviors the dominant dog will most likely exhibit.

Your Dog Is Driven to Exploit You

Every species evolves to maximize opportunities for survival, and your cute, loving shih tzu is no different. Society has perpetuated the belief that dogs are kind, loving animals whose only joy in life is to satisfy humans and lavish us with unconditional love. While this is a more pleasurable scenario to imagine, in fact your sweet pup is trying to exploit you so that she gets what *she* wants. After you get over the initial hurt of this concept, there's some good news: by understanding this dynamic, it becomes simple to nurture the perfect VBD.

Dogs are hardwired to extract as many resources from us as possible. Food, water, and shelter are the basics, but these days the spoils of domesticity include top-notch medical care, expensive organic diets, plush bedding, art-quality chew toys, and doting care at luxury kennels. All they have to do in return is make us believe that they love us—and, of course, misbehave.

How did this species exploit us so obviously and yet so insidiously? Easy. First, wild dogs and wolves who weren't fearful of humans—often runts abandoned by their packs—crawled up to us at the campfire to beg for scraps and crumbs, manifesting submissive obeisance. Over time, as shown by the Russian scientist Dmitri Belyaev, the interbreeding

VBD Hall of Fame: Paw-to-Mouth

Talk about a food drive! For these pooches, mere kibble would never be enough.

- British bullmastiff Deefer likes his panties. Or make that women's panties, including thongs; Deefer has expressed no interest in men's underwear. After safely consuming 20 pairs in a year, 3 particularly frilly pairs lodged in his intestines and had to be removed surgically. Fortunately, his family, aware of his habit, had previously invested in pet insurance.

- Upon realizing that two $100 bills had disappeared from her coat pocket, a Pennsylvania woman had no idea who the culprit might be—until she cleaned up after her Doberman pinscher, Mia, and found telltale pieces of green paper. Over 24 hours, this proud owner removed the bits of bills from Mia's every poop, then exchanged the remnants for fresh money at her local bank.

- Another Brit, Lulu the Labrador, became a suspect when her owner's expensive Gucci watch went missing. An X-ray located the watch, still ticking, and after a quick operation the watch (functional, albeit slightly damaged by stomach acid) was recovered along with a missing sock.

of these self-selected canines resulted in surprising genetic shifts. They wagged their tails and licked humans to demonstrate affection. Their ears became floppy, their tails curled, and their coats developed spots. In short, they became cute.

One aspect of VBD behavior, as outlined in chapter 1, is canine freedom of choice—allowing your dog to express her innate dogness, released from the constraints of the expectations for the modern dog. Drives are a significant aspect of the authentic inner dog that you will allow to reemerge. Like a Michelangelo pulling *David* out of the block of marble, so will you provide the freedom for your dog to become who she really is.

Understanding Drives

Inherited drives dictate a dog's personality because they define what is intrinsically satisfying to her. Drives are even more influential than intelligence, which for dogs is generally characterized as problem-solving ability. Understanding the seven drives that come into play with dogs will equip you to identify your dog's strengths and weaknesses when it comes to poor behaviors so that you can point her in the right direction.

What Motivates Your Dog? Bringing Out the Worst

To make it as easy and satisfying as possible for your dog to learn and enjoy ill behaviors, you'll need to observe your pet and find out what makes her tick. Most dogs display tendencies toward one drive over others. Identifying that dominant drive will make it easier to train poor behaviors that are associated with that drive. For example, a dog with a high social drive will want to be around other social beings (human or canine) more than anything else. For this dog, effusive greeting behaviors that manifest themselves as hyperactivity and jumping up are easy to encourage. A dog with a low prey drive but a high defensive drive would make a poor candidate for a cat chaser, but she could very easily be encouraged to become an ankle biter. Once you have identified your dog's dominant drives, you can begin to think about ways to nurture them and set your dog up for VBD success.

Drive	Definition	Manifestation	Associated VBD Behavior
Food	Desire to eat.	Snacking, ingesting kibble.	Stealing food.
Sex	Desire to copulate. (Diminished in spayed or neutered dogs.)	Trying to have sex with other dogs.	Escaping to hunt down the ladies.
Prey	Desire to chase and kill prey.	Chasing small furry animals and shaking them violently.	Chasing cars.
Defense	Desire to protect self, pack, and territory.	Barking, growling, snapping, biting.	Biting the mailman.
Hunt	Desire to look for prey when it is out of sight.	Relentlessly searching for lost objects.	Obsessive-compulsive tendencies.
Social	Desire for social acceptance and harmony.	Gregarious behaviors, excessive tail wagging, need to be with others.	Jumping on strangers, separation anxiety.
Dominance	Desire to dominate other pack members.	Fighting. Guarding food and other valued objects.	Aggression around the food dish.

VBD Indigestion

Pica, an endlessly entertaining dog neurosis, is the propensity for ingesting inedibles, including the following documented objects that required medical treatment:

Battery*	Golf ball*	Plastic chicken
Cell phone	Hearing aid	Pool ball
Cigarette lighter	iPod*	Razor blade
Condom*	Kebob skewer*	Scissors
Diaper*	Magnet	Tampon*
Fake excrement	Marijuana	Vibrator*
Glass eye*	Metal fork	Videotape

*Multiple items swallowed by the same dog.

Food Dog

A dog with a high food drive will:

- Seek out food to the exclusion of all other outside stimuli.

- Drool incessantly when presented with the opportunity to eat.

- Wolf down food—it's all good.

- Snap at the hand that feeds her, in order to swallow food more quickly.

- Respond quickly to any visible treat, and often present different behaviors (sitting, rolling over, barking) for more.

- Eat to excess.

Of course, all dogs have the food drive, but some dogs focus on food with undistractable intent. If your dog is a food dog, she will succeed at begging, stealing food, counter-surfing, and foraging.

Sex Dog

A dog with a high sex drive will:

- Hump other dogs, legs, and inanimate objects, such as stuffed animals.

- Whine or cry when in the presence of female dogs in heat.

- Show aggression toward other male dogs but not necessarily female ones.

If your male dog is intact (not neutered; see "Dog as Compensation for Inadequacy" in chapter 2), then he will have a naturally high sex drive. A sexed-out dog will excel at escaping the yard, running away to chase after females, refusing to come when called, and dog-on-dog aggression.

Prey Dog

A dog with a high prey drive will:

- Show a huge interest in small furry objects and animals.

- Stalk birds; chase cats.

- Chase bicycles, skateboards, and cars.

- Chase with vigor and glee after tennis balls and other tossed toys.

- Shake and "kill" stuffed toys.

- Instigate games by shoving toys in your lap.

If you have a prey-driven dog, you are one lucky owner. The prey drive leads to all sorts of ill behaviors. Your dog will be a superstar at

chasing and killing small wildlife; chasing cars;
dog-on-dog aggression (directed toward smaller
dogs); and excessive destruction inside the house.
A select group of highly driven prey dogs will
develop obsessive fetching behaviors. A prey
dog may or may not also have the hunt drive
(see page 63), while the hunt dog will always have
the prey drive.

Defense Dog

A dog with a high defense drive will:

- Show a distrust of strangers, often cringing
  from contact.

- Run up to unknown people, nip their ankles
  or legs, and then immediately retreat.

- Bare teeth, growl, or snap when backed into a corner, especially by people she doesn't like.

- Bark ferociously at people or dogs when on the leash during walks.

- Bark at passersby while in the car, regardless of their appearance and whether they pose a credible threat to the automobile.

- Guard the house relentlessly, often engaging in diligent perimeter control to make sure security has not been breached.

- Misbehave during visits to the vet or groomer.

It is incredibly easy to manipulate a highly defensive dog to bring out the worst behaviors; this quality is thus highly desirable in the VBD. A dog who naturally fears and suspects the unknown easily learns to growl at and bite strangers, chase the mail carrier, attack trespassing animals, snap at children, bark incessantly, and develop neurotic behaviors.

Hunt Dog

A dog with a high hunt drive will:

- Unnaturally fixate on tennis balls or other retrievable objects.

- Perceive light beams (from a mirror or flashlight) as prey.

- Search for hours for lizards, squirrels, cats, rodents, or other living creatures that may be inhabiting your backyard.

- Destroy such objects as your couch that stand between her and her toys.

- Stalk birds with incredible stealth and patience.

Hunting dogs tend to focus on lost objects, which leads them to excel at interior home destruction. These noble animals will also exhibit neurotic behaviors, which manifest themselves as self-mutilation, obsessive-compulsive rituals, refusing to come when called, and standoffishness toward owners. As noted previously, a hunting dog will always have the prey drive as well.

Social Dog

A dog with a high social drive will:

- Love other dogs to excess.

Doggy Dictionary: Peternity Leave

When you get your new VBD, make sure you demand "peternity leave," time off from work to bond. Also called "puppy leave."

- Enjoy dog parks, doggy day care, and other social venues more than anything.

- Show enormous amounts of excitement at meeting new people, dogs, and other animals.

- Greet the world vigorously with the notion that all people and dogs will be in their fan club.

- Love to go to the vet or groomer.

- Jump up on anyone that comes to the door.

- Pull on the leash to hail strangers.

Social dogs are the most common dogs today. While it may be difficult to instill certain poor behaviors more typical of the other drives, there are still plenty of social impulses that can be harnessed for chaos. A dog who is highly social craves your attention and affection and therefore succeeds at separation anxiety, effusive greeting, hyperactivity, drooling, jumping up, pulling on the leash, barking, and begging.

Dominance Dog

A dog with a high dominance drive will:

- Bully other dogs for position at the door or food dish.

- Take valued objects or treats from other dogs by growling.

- Will meet and greet other dogs with an upright, stiff posture and a high tail carriage.

- Will physically dominate her owner by pushing or leaning.

- Will guard her own objects against any and all approaching "threats."

- Will control her household by using violence— growling, snapping, or biting—to get what she wants.

It's easy to foster VBD behavior in the dominant dog: be passive and allow the dog to do whatever she wants. A dominant dog is best suited for territorial aggression, biting or snapping at her owner, fighting over the food dish, fighting with other dogs, general disobedience, and pulling on the leash.

The VBD Drive

Now that you've identified the basic drives in your dog, you'll be able to focus on developing the very bad behaviors that are associated with your dog's drives, and learning will be faster and more satisfying for both of you. Bear in mind that all dogs have behaviors associated with all the drives, and most dogs are dominant in more than one drive. The trick is to harness your dog's primary drives and exploit them. With a dog who exhibits the characteristics of many drives, the VBD possibilities are endless.

Now that you know what kind of owner you are, why dogs are the way they are, and what kind of dog you have, it's time to start with actual behavioral modification. In chapter 5, you'll learn how to approach your relationship with your dog, setting up the foundation for VBD development.

THE SIX VBD
CORNERSTONES

5
ESTABLISHING THE FOUNDATION

Before any dog tricks or specific behaviors are reinforced by human interaction, a relationship develops between person and pet, with behavior-reaction dynamics that the dog quickly learns to identify. When it comes to cultivating a VBD there are shortcuts and long detours, easy and labor-intensive approaches. By absorbing the six cornerstones of the VBD philosophy, you will fluidly nurture your VBD in your day-to-day life with minimal time and effort. If you follow our easy principles, you'll soon find that your dog is *naturally* becoming more and more ill-behaved.

In this chapter, you'll learn the secrets to the VBD, including:

- The six cornerstones of the VBD philosophy: dominance permission, inconsistency, confusion, ineffectual repetition, anthropomorphism, and lack of exercise.

- Why consistency is the hobgoblin of little minds.

- Whether it's better for one person or several to cultivate your VBD.

- How to foster complete indifference to commands.

Give Dominance Permission

The sooner you give up your notion of control over your dog, the more success you will have in your VBD quest. This idea is counterintuitive in a society that feels dogs should be subservient to humans, but life is far more interesting when a dog is making the decisions.

To accomplish this, remind yourself that he is in charge, not you. Your job as owner is to provide him with as many opportunities for dominance as possible. Encourage him to experiment with a variety of dominance behaviors, including jumping all over

VBD Insurance

As a VBD owner, you want to make sure that your dog is covered by your homeowner's or renter's insurance. When you're protected from the financial burden of property damage as well as the inevitable, probably well-deserved bite, your dog can run free on his path to destruction while you sit back and enjoy it.

Dog bites are welcome business for insurance companies, accounting for as much as 25 percent of all liability claims and 6 percent of claim costs. More than 4.7 million people are bitten each year; about 20 percent need medical attention. Over half of dog-bite victims are children.

To make sure you're covered, request a $2 million umbrella policy to cover liability for your car and house. This excessive coverage will cost you a bit more, but at least you'll be protected should Fido take a nip out of the mailman.

you, pulling and lunging on the leash, guarding food, and humping. Humping, while often misinterpreted as a sexual behavior, is usually a sign of dominance. The dog is really saying, "Take that!" If your dog shows an interest in humping you, your leg, or your guests, push him away meekly, being careful not to actually dislodge him. The timid effort will encourage him to be more forceful in his dominance displays.

One common mistake made by novice VBD owners stems from the belief that dogs engage in certain behaviors, such as climbing onto the furniture, out of love or a desire to be near you. Your dog may love you, but first and foremost, he wants to control you and your resources, and you need to make sure you allow that. An excellent way to reinforce your dog's sense of self-importance is allowing him to choose and control where he sleeps. Naturally, he'll choose your bed, and, with any luck, will have you sleeping at the very edge while he takes over the prime central real estate— under the covers, of course. In the case of couples, allow him to sleep in between the two of you.

Other ways to foster dominance include:

- Feeding him before you eat, while you watch.

- Giving in to all demands for food or treats, including limitless samples of your own snacks or meals.

- Allowing him complete access to furniture, throws, and pillows. If he's a small dog, make sure you provide him a way to jump up, such as a stack of books for a makeshift stairway.

- Giving him first choice as to where he hangs out. If you're in his way, move.

- Letting him decide where he goes on his walks, as well as what he sniffs and for how long.

- Allowing him to guard any favorite objects, including other family members. If he growls when you approach, back off.

Practice Inconsistency Inconsistently

Because dogs learn obedience through consistency, this tired approach is the sacred cow of obedience training. Life is more fun, however, with an unpredictable dog. A dog that jumps out of car windows, disappears for days at a time, or rearranges your decor on an ongoing basis is ripe fodder for those little anecdotes we all love to tell. Varied and developed behaviors will spring, almost magically, from inconsistency.

To avoid being consistent, follow these tenets:

- Always practice inconsistency, but not consistently. Never do the same thing twice, except sometimes. Make sure your dog's day is full of surprises.

- If ever you want your dog to do something specific, vary the command words: "Sit!" could just as easily be phrased as "Fido, take a load off." You can even speak to your dog in different languages.

The Miracle of Anthropomorphism

Anthropomorphism—attributing human characteristics to nonhuman animals—is an ideal way to approach your dog. If this were not the case, Cassius Marcellus Coolidge's paintings of dogs playing poker would not have been so popular for more than a hundred years.

When you interact with your dog, assume he has emotions and feelings exactly the same as yours. After all, *he* believes that *you* think like a dog. Theories suggest that domesticated animals who don't provide food, labor, or material goods—so-called social parasites—evolved a "cute response" to elicit our parental instincts. Wouldn't it stand to reason that they would also evolve such emotions as guilt, remorse, and jealousy? (Not that VBDs, of course, *should* ever feel these things.)

Aesthetically, dogs are bred specially for human qualities, with expressive faces—all the better to be dressed and coddled. Why not interpret their actions as smiles, pouts, or hugs? Or imagine they understand the passage of time and abstract cause and effect? After all, not only is anthropomorphism easier than interspecies understanding, it's also more effective at eliciting very bad behavior.

- Change the rules as often as you can, then don't enforce them. If he never knows the rules, they're very easy for him to break!

Multilayered Confusion

Ideally, several different people will participate in handling your dog. Varied influences will naturally create an aversion in your dog to any particular behavior, injecting his life with a healthy degree of confusion. When your dog is disoriented, he's much more likely to engage in behaviors that he himself finds fulfilling. You'll want to give him many choices for activities so he can select his own path, as a dog with a vast array of options ("What should I chew *now*?") will undoubtedly choose the most ill-behaved ones.

Consistent with the concept of inconsistency, make sure that every member of your household has different rules and expectations from your dog. By providing your dog with many cues, none of them similar, you avoid accidentally teaching your dog to be obedient. For example, make sure that "Come!" is not actively enforced in the traditional sense.

Once your dog has cleverly avoided a narrow interpretation of a command in favor of a broader—and more optional—one, he will develop his own versions, a great foundation for bad behavior.

Other commands that lend themselves to multiple interpretations include:

- **Heel:** Different household members should walk your dog differently—one person with the dog on the right side, one on the left, one with a very long leash, etc. One should allow the dog to sniff, the other should pull him along.

- **Down:** Because *down* can mean both "Lie down!" and "Stop jumping!" this command is great for families. Use it in both ways, inconsistently. Remember, too, that *lie down* can mean, "Put all of your body parts on the ground," "Roll over and recline to the side," or "Roll over on your back and grab the leash in your mouth."

> ### 💬 Canine Quip
>
> *"Dogs are the leaders of the planet. If you see two life forms, one of them's making a poop, the other one's carrying it for him, who would you assume is in charge?"*
>
> **—Jerry Seinfeld**

Ineffectual Repetition for Feigned Indifference

Feigned indifference goes hand in hand with inconsistency and is the result of ineffectual repetition. If you observe successful VBD owners, you'll see that they repeat to their dogs: "sit-sit-sit-SIT!" Their dogs have already learned that if they don't sit on the first command, nothing happens. If there is no consequence to disobedience then the dog is free to pursue his own interests. Thus the dog pretends he has absolutely no idea what *sit* actually means.

When addressing your dog, therefore, make sure you repeat commands over and over again. Soon "Sit!" will have no more impact on your dog than

"Noodles!" Your dog may or may not choose to sit when asked. Foster this thought process when developing a VBD.

You also want to cultivate your dog's feigned indifference to his own name. An obedience-trained dog will, upon hearing his name, swivel his head toward the voice calling him, as if to say, "What?" On the contrary, the correct VBD response is complete ignorance. To cultivate this, repeat the dog's name in such a way that he soon becomes immune to it ("Fido, Fido, Fido, Fido, Fido," followed by no discernible action) or implement a host of nicknames so your dog is never really sure what his name actually is.

Pro-Anthropomorphism

When approaching the VBD, you must convince yourself that he possesses human thoughts and emotions. While intellectually we know that dogs are not human, psychologically we cannot divorce ourselves from the idea that the codependence we foster is reciprocally fulfilling. Many people truly believe that their dogs empathize on a deeper, human level. Whether or not this is true is irrelevant. The important thing is to treat your dog like a human in order to create a host of behavior problems.

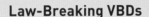

Law-Breaking VBDs

There's a small legal industry geared toward restricting the rights of your VBD. From leash laws to pooper-scooper regulations, a small group of antidog citizens have imposed their preferences on the rest of us.

Leash laws actually work somewhat in the VBD's favor. Because they feel cornered, dogs tend to be more aggressive when *on* a leash than when allowed to walk freely! Additionally, most dog bites occur on private property, often within the owner's home or yard.

When it comes to pooper-scooper laws, most people would agree that the job of cleaning up 2 million tons of dog feces annually in the United States is better performed by cities and gardeners. Besides—how hard is it to wash off a shoe?

By projecting your own feelings onto your dog, you'll be able to reinterpret standard canine behavior. For example, at least half of the owners of rescued dogs claim their dog was abused. While certainly some dogs have experienced terrible treatment, the cringing that dogs display when voices or hands are raised is a completely normal canine response of submission. Nevertheless, we continue to explicate canine behavior as human, and in doing so, we begin to *treat* the dog like a human (an equal or superior, as in the "Give Dominance Permission" section) as well as misunderstand what the dog actually needs, thus fostering poor behavior.

Other anthropomorphic misinterpretations include:

- **Dogs understand time.** Dogs do not register the passage of time like people do. Believing that your dog misses you more if you're gone longer will result in more effusive displays of affection on your part when you return, thus laying the groundwork for a good case of separation anxiety.

- **Dogs understand democracy.** Dogs work in a strictly hierarchical social system. If there is more than one dog in the household, treating both dogs as equals will successfully blur the status lines between them, leading to squabbling over food, treats, and toys, as well as the development of excessive dominance, which will usually manifest itself in some type of aggression.

- **Dogs need to engage in sex.** Dogs are often left unneutered because owners believe that their pets need to engage in sexual activity for complete fulfillment. Intact dogs leave the door open for many VBD behaviors, and many more VBDs.

- **Dogs don't enjoy regular dog food.** Throughout history, dogs have been scavengers, eating only leftovers at irregular intervals. When a dog is believed to be human, food suddenly becomes much more important. Owners begin to cater to the dog's gustatory whims just as they would for a fussy child, which results in extremely selective eating habits.

Never Exercise Your Dog

By walking or running your dog, playing fetch or Frisbee, or hiring a dog walker, you waste valuable physical and emotional energy that is better directed toward poor behavior. A well-exercised dog tends to lounge about the house doing very little when he isn't involved in his daily activity—not a prime example of a VBD, to be sure.

A Solid Foundation for Poor Behavior

The six pillars on which the VBD philosophy proudly rests will serve you throughout your VBD journey, no matter which specific behaviors you choose to cultivate. When combined with principles of reward and deterrent, the subject of the next chapter, these basic principles will allow you to point your dog in any VBD direction.

VERY BAD
BEHAVIOR
MODIFICATION

 6

REWARDS AND DETERRENTS

Basic behavior theory works on many species,
including spouses. Here, however, we want to
apply its tools toward developing a successful
VBD. In order to do this, you need to understand
how behavior is shaped. These tools are no
different from those used in traditional obedience
training; they are just applied differently, and
more pleasurably at that.

Behavioral modification is accomplished by a
combination of positive reinforcement, which is
rewarding a behavior (for example, with food)
in order to increase it and positive punishment
(also called negative reinforcement), which is

correcting unwanted behavior via an aversive (such as a sharp leash correction) in order to decrease it. Finally, ignoring an unwanted behavior functions to extinguish it.

While it seems a bit theoretical at this point, don't worry—we'll give you the concrete tools you need, including lessons such as:

- Recognizing nonfood rewards for your dog.

- Harnessing the power of unpredictability.

- Limiting inadvertent rewards that encourage obedience.

- Using the powerful jackpot theory of variable rewards.

Positive Reinforcement to Encourage Poor Behavior

With behavior theory, you want to reward behaviors that you like, because every reward will increase the likelihood that it will occur again.

Retractable Leashes for VBDs

There is no better piece of equipment for the VBD than the retractable leash. This innovation consists of a thin nylon line, generally 15 to 18 feet long, that spring-coils out of a plastic housing. A button provides "brakes."

Retractable leashes give VBDs freedom, a huge radius within which they can eat inappropriate objects, jump on strangers, and attack approaching dogs. The thin nylon line is impossible to grab in urgent situations, nor can you effectively reel it in. Unlike with a standard leash, you don't run the risk of accidentally punishing poor behavior with a collar correction. Finally, retractable leashes cause severe rope burns to bystanders who get in the way of your VBD's high-speed chases.

Dogs generally repeat behaviors that feel good, taste good, or accomplish a goal.

Rewards for your dog aren't confined to food treats. Destruction sessions (ripping apart pillows), freedom (bolting out the door), and prey pursuits (chasing the cat) could be intrinsically rewarding for your dog, depending on her personality. In chapter 4, you identified what motivates your dog, and indeed the key to reinforcing very bad behavior is to identify what is of high value for your dog then to provide those experiences or items when she behaves badly.

Reward #1: Things That Feel Good

The number-one reason a dog repeats a behavior is because it feels good to her. This could be a fond pat on the head, but more likely it's something that feels good on a much deeper level. The pursuit of your dog's drives feel good to her. For example, a social dog will feel best when she's engaged in social interactions, so you'll want to greet her effusively when she jumps on you even if you are simultaneously saying "Off!" in a friendly tone of voice. Keep in mind that some dogs respond quite well to any attention, even what we sometimes call "negative attention"—yelling, pushing, or chasing. These types of responses are often interpreted by your dog as an invitation to play, and thus can be considered a reward for poor behavior.

Reward #2: Things That Taste Good

All dogs can be rewarded with things that taste good.

Providing a tidbit or treat (or big juicy steak) will always reinforce a poor behavior.

Reward #3: Things That Accomplish a Goal

A dog who's trying to achieve something (and remember, what he is trying to achieve depends on his drives) will experiment with different tactics. Whichever tactic is successful will be repeated. For example, if your dog wants to come inside, he will first scratch at the door, then bark, then whine, etc. Reward all of these behaviors by opening the door.

Discouraging Unwanted Behavior

When your dog performs in a way you don't like—for example, if she sits or stays on command—you will want to correct it with an aversive, which is essentially the opposite of a reward. Dogs avoid behaviors that feel bad, are frightening or unpredictable, or don't accomplish goals. Inflicting aversives is no fun, so fortunately they're rarely necessary to attain the VBD, one of the many pleasures of this approach.

Persuading the Mailman to Leave

Have you ever wondered why dogs seem to hate the mailman? Many believe it's the uniform, but that detail comes after the fact. Here's how it works: mail carriers come every day, around the same time, and invade the property. Due to the incredibly convincing defense mounted by your dog, the carrier leaves. Your dog believes that it's his barking, growling, and spinning that deters the mailman from sticking around. Your dog is intelligently repeating behaviors that accomplish a daily goal: get the guy in the funny trousers to leave.

This is no joke to the post office. In 2004, the Canadian pet chain Pet Valu began carrying Bark Bars, dog treats shaped like mail carriers. The Canada Post—which documents some 300 dog attacks per year—protested, and Pet Valu voluntarily pulled the treats.

Aversive #1: Things That Feel Bad

This is probably the most common method for obedience training. There are many aversive obedience-training products on the market, ranging from choke chains to electric fences. Understandably, dogs don't repeat behaviors that cause them pain or discomfort, but why would you want to cause your dog pain or discomfort?

Aversive #2: Unpredictable Things

Dogs like predictable reactions from everyday objects. Loud, startling noises or sudden movements can be frightening. For example, the sound of a glass breaking or the motion of an umbrella opening terrifies dogs, who don't expect inanimate objects to behave this way. You'll want to be careful to avoid these types of unpredictable situations for two reasons: one, she won't be desensitized to her fears and will become increasingly anxious, possibly phobic; and two, you don't want to discourage certain types of poor behavior. For example, if your dog jumps to retrieve the bacon that's been left on the counter and accidentally sends a platter flying across the floor, shattering noisily into a hundred pieces, she may never eat off the counter again.

Aversive #3:
Things That Don't Accomplish Goals

A dog will soon abandon behaviors that don't accomplish goals. If your dog is trying to get you to pet her by nudging your elbow with her nose, and that doesn't work, she'll up the ante by squeezing her entire head under your arm, cycling through different tactics until she finds one that works. Rather than ignoring her, which could serve to extinguish the behaviors, you'll want to show her that many different such behaviors will accomplish her desired goals.

Recognizing Inadvertent Rewards and Punishments

Remember those dog owners who, without seeming to lift a finger, have perfect VBDs? Chances are they both increase rewards and limit punishments without any idea that they're doing so. With this in mind, you'll need to be careful that you don't accidentally reward behaviors you don't want reinforced. For example, if you absentmindedly hand your dog a cookie while she's sitting still— or worse, treat her for promptly answering your call to come—she might do it again. You don't want to be faced with an obedient dog, so make sure to reward deliberately.

Recognizing and limiting possible punishments is even trickier. Many poor behaviors are instinctively punished. For example, a dog who bites the postman might get kicked in return, thereby making her cautious of nipping others in the future. A dog who pulls on the leash might receive an unintentional collar correction. Care must be exercised to avoid these potential aversives or your dog may choose to avoid very bad behaviors altogether.

The Power of Variable Reward: The "Jackpot" Theory

Ever wonder why the slots in Vegas are so popular? People are lured to them for the possibility of a big reward. They drop in quarter after quarter, hoping to hit it big. They're rewarded every so often with a small token, just enough to keep them interested. "If I keep doing this," they think, "sooner or later I'll get the big prize."

Your dog's mind works in the same way. In order to make a behavior stick, you have to convince your dog that every so often she'll get something fantastically great—if she keeps working at it.

In the meantime, you must keep her interested with a series of randomly spaced, small rewards until she hits the jackpot. This is called "variable reward" because the intervals between the rewards vary.

The "jackpot" is the be-all and end-all of rewards. Make sure your dog "jackpots" at least once for every poor behavior you are trying to instill, and she'll never forget it. For example, a dog who's been fed once from the table will continue begging for years without results, until one night when the polite but vegetarian Aunt Sally comes to visit and feeds the dog her steak under the table—jackpot!

It's a VBD-Eat-VBD World

The phrase "dog-eat-dog" actually derives from its opposite. The Latin proverb *Canis caninam non est* (a dog does not eat dog's flesh) underscored the natural limits of brutality. The saying traveled to English as "Dog does not eat dog" and in the eighteenth century inverted into "Dogs are hard drove, when they eat dogs."

Reward Yourself with a VBD

It takes some discipline to be sure that you're rewarding the poor behaviors you want and averting the obedience that you don't, but after the initial learning period, you'll be impressed by the extent to which your dog is able to take your shoe and run with it. It all comes down to mindfulness— be aware of the signals you're sending your dog so that you can deliberately shape her poor behavior.

Now that you understand the broad strokes of canine psychology, it's time to start tackling some actual behaviors. In chapter 7, we're going to put your newfound knowledge to work.

BEGINNING VBD SKILLS

7

NO BOUNDARIES ALLOWED

Welcome to the section of the book you probably thought we were going to start with—actual very bad behaviors and how to instill them. Hopefully you now see, however, how important it was to cover all the fundamentals. With those tools, even if the behaviors we outline aren't the ones you desire, you'll be able to figure out a way to develop those you do seek.

While chapter 8 outlines more advanced behaviors, chapter 7 focuses on the early development of the VBD: boundaries, housebreaking, socialization, and destruction, all rich breeding grounds for poor behavior. Even if you're starting with an adult dog rather than a puppy, you can still backtrack to instill some of these basic behaviors. Among the many things you will learn in this chapter are:

- Why you should never crate your dog.

- How failing to housebreak will greatly improve your immunity.

- How to transmit your social nervousness to your pup.

- Why to call your dog when he doesn't want to come.

The Myth of the Dog Cave

A particularly nasty myth has circulated among obedience trainers over the last two decades: the idea that dogs like to be crated. These self-proclaimed experts claim that dogs enjoy crates because they are "den-like" and dogs, after all, are den animals. Though it may be difficult to get the dog to use his crate at first, the party line goes, soon enough he'll willingly enter the crate and actually prefer it.

Where There's a Will

Why leave your earthly riches to your VBD? Since pets are considered property, and property can't own property, pets cannot legally inherit money. While there are no national laws around estate planning for pets, 35 states have enacted legislation recognizing their legality. Some one million Americans have designated their pets as beneficiaries, with the average bequest around $25,000. Some individuals even leave instructions and funds for their pet to be relocated to "retirement communities," luxury resorts where pets can live out the rest of their owner-free days.

Rich dogs are the stuff of both legends and truth; Gunther the Alsatian shepherd's hundreds of millions of dollars, for example, may be apocryphal. Doris Duke left her dog $100,000, while actress Betty White has reportedly willed all to her pets. A British mutt named Jasper controls almost $300,000 and has the run of his own thirteenth-century estate.

With a VBD, you might want to speak to an attorney about protecting your pooch from liability issues—deep pockets and poor behavior may be a bad combination.

Nothing could be further from the truth. Give any dog the choice of a crate or a down-filled comforter on a Posturepedic with human company, and he'll always choose the latter. Who are the crates for then? Humans! Some owners want time apart from their dogs or want to limit household access, especially when they aren't at home.

We're not concerned with *who* desires the crate: our priority is that crating disrupts VBD goals. The best VBDs don't have any boundaries. They go where they want, when they want. You don't want to teach your dog to "be comfortably alone" or "take a time out," as the obedience nonsense states. These dynamics will infringe on your dog's ingenuity and take away from his necessary experience seeking out entertainment in your home. If your dog isn't used to crate-like environments, if he ever does find himself in such a situation, he'll make plenty of noise, the healthy canine reaction.

Finally, crates limit the amount of damage your dog can inflict on your household. Why would you want to do that?

Housebreaking Is Overrated

Limiting your dog's elimination habits is not only time consuming for you, it runs counter to natural canine behavior. In the wild, wolves may not do their business near where they sleep, but everywhere else is fair game. Dogs are no different. They want the freedom to go whenever, wherever. No dog chooses to be housebroken.

If dogs had their druthers, they would mark their territory, which of course includes your house. (This has the added advantage of preventing strange dogs from approaching your home without trepidation.) Most dog owners only housebreak their dogs because they've been taught that dog waste is filthy and unhygienic. However, there is a belief in the scientific community that exposure to healthy bacteria is actually beneficial in building immunity to illnesses and disease.

If you do choose to housebreak, be sure to practice such ineffective means of reinforcement as rubbing your dog's face in his mess or scolding him after the fact. Those reactions do nothing to further the cause of housebreaking but tend to promote poor behavior, so you may come out ahead. And if the cleanup really bothers you, use dog diapers. These are sold in two models: a "belly band" for males and undergarment-style panties for females. As you can imagine, your dog will really enjoy wearing them.

Socializing a Puppy

A poorly socialized puppy will turn into a fearful, nervous adult—a truly desirable VBD profile. A dog that has little or no exposure to new sounds, new scents, and new sights, not to mention new people and other dogs, will naturally have a higher defensive drive than a dog who's been paraded all over town. The high defense drive is critical in developing barking, growling, and snapping behaviors.

> 💬 **Canine Quip**
>
> *"A door is what a dog is perpetually on the wrong side of."*
>
> **—Ogden Nash**

Dogs also pick up on the emotions of their owners. When with your dog, be fearful as others approach. Pull him off to the side or pick him up to let them pass. When he growls or cowers, pet him to reinforce his behavior (make it look like you are just soothing him). If he barks and lunges, get down to his level and say, "There, there" as you stroke his brow, as if calming him down. With this kind of positive reinforcement, he'll repeat these behaviors in no time!

On the other hand, if your dog has a high social drive, you'll want to encourage this enviable lack of boundaries. Dogs greet one another by jumping up, mouthing and licking at each other's faces, and running around excitedly, yapping and barking. These are natural behaviors, which become even more charming in full-grown dogs. If you have a puppy, make sure that you don't accidentally discourage these greeting rituals with harsh words, leash corrections, or refusing to pay attention. Instead, receive your dog warmly and enthusiastically when he jumps onto your best suit when you come home from work, or pretend to swat him away, murmuring "No" and his name so he can enjoy that game. When guests come to visit, don't put your dog into a sit-stay when they arrive. He's your best ambassador, so let him loose!

Dog-on-Dog Etiquette

Places such as the dog park provide excellent environments for instilling poor social behavior in your dog. When teaching your dog how to play with others, you can go in one of two ways: turning your dog into a sissy or a bully.

From the time they can walk, puppies engage in play fighting. These behaviors establish dominance, teach bite inhibition, and encourage good social skills, whereby a dog learns how to avoid fights by exhibiting the proper cues of dominance and submission. Because this is not your goal as the owner of a VBD, you'll need to countercondition your pup to play rough. To do this, pair him with an older, larger dog that will bully him (active dogs in the twelve-to-eighteen-month-old range are a good choice) then let them roughhouse. If a fight ensues, don't break it up. Instead, let them hash it out and learn that fighting solves every squabble. Cheering your dog on will further cement this behavior.

On the other hand, if your dog is timid and you are a nervous Nellie, interfere in his play in order to inhibit his social skills. While dogs growl and vocalize even during the friendliest of wrestling matches, assume that every sound is a sign that your precious pooch is about to be killed. Jump in prematurely, call his name repeatedly, and pull him away from the other dogs. When he attempts to return to his buddies, repeat the process.

Walking the Human

Walking nicely on a leash—or heeling, as it's sometimes called—is one of more difficult behaviors to properly obedience train. It's therefore no surprise that one of the easiest poor behaviors to cultivate is walking poorly on a leash. After all, most dogs do it naturally. They are far more interested in what's going on around them than they are in keeping pace with your stride. Bugs, grass, squirrels, birds—a walk offers up myriad sniffing opportunities, and your dog should be encouraged to investigate them all, for however long he wants.

The most important thing to remember on walks is that your dog is in charge, not you. He chooses the direction, speed, and intensity. From the very beginning of the excursion, he should lead the way, walking through doors and gates before you. He'll soon lead you to fascinating places you'd never see on your own, like alleyways, garbage piles, and gutters. Along the way, make sure that he's allowed to greet in his own fashion whatever traffic you may encounter. Whether he is aggressive or effusive, part of the joy of a daily walk lies in meeting others.

Of course you'll want him to pull on the leash—this is how he tells you where he wants to go and shows you that he's a spirited canine. Just run to keep up with him and get cortisone shots in your elbow if necessary.

Doggy High Tech

For the dog owner who loves to buy the latest gadgets, there's plenty out there for your VBD.

- **For the escape artist:** Let your dog escape with impunity: try VBD GPS, the Global Pet Finder collar.

- **For the neurotic:** Strap the Pet's Eye View camera onto your dog's collar; it snaps pictures at automatic intervals. At the end of the day, download the shots to see what seems to freak him out. That way, you can make sure there's no end to it!

- **For the prey-driven:** Chasing the Go-Go Dog Pal—a remote-control-squirrel dog toy—will soon encourage attacks on any small, roving creature, from kitties to toddlers!

- **For the narcissist:** Thanks to an electronic collar, the Power Pet Electronic Dog Door will open whenever your pooch approaches, helpfully confirming that the world revolves around her needs.

Coming When Called: Breaking a Bad Habit

Most puppies are hardwired to come when called, but fortunately they tend to outgrow this nasty habit at about four months old. If for some reason your dog still comes when called when he's past the young puppy stage, implement the following steps to nip this behavior in the bud:

1. **Call your dog when he doesn't want to come.** Wait until your dog is completely engrossed in something, like playing with another dog at the dog park or barking at the mailman. After you're sure that there's no chance he'll actually choose you over the object of his attention, say, "Come!" in a demanding, angry voice. If he ignores you, good: you've just taught him that "Come!" means "You don't have to come."

2. **If, by accident, he does come, ignore him completely.** Don't pet him, don't praise him, and don't make eye contact with him no matter how much he wants your attention. Refrain from any

interaction with him until he wanders off. Then wait five minutes and call him again.

3. **Call your dog when you have to do something unpleasant.** Make sure you call your dog to come immediately before you do something he dislikes, such as taking him to the vet or clipping his toenails. Hopefully he'll begin to associate the word *come* with things he'd like to avoid and soon run to hide in response.

Doggy Dictionary: Latchkey Dog

The term for a dog who is left home alone and unsupervised all day to cultivate VBD behavior.

4. **Teach your dog that the command "Come" precedes a game of catch-me.** If you call your dog and he doesn't come, run after him. Chasing games are very fun for dogs, particularly when they are unleashed in public around heavy traffic. Screaming "Come!" louder and louder as he slips from your grasp increases the excitement and effectiveness of the game.

Ball of Destruction

If you don't encourage destruction in your VBD, not only will he fail to achieve his full dogness, you will not experience the benefit of freedom of detachment from material possessions. An adventuresome dog is a happy dog. Dogs who are encouraged to creatively explore their environments are healthier and more contented, and at times this resourcefulness will include destructive behavior.

The best way to encourage creative canine play is to treat all household objects as your dog's possession. There should be no distinguishing factor between what is and isn't his. Remember, it's *all* his. Your dog should be encouraged to believe that everything in the house is fair game. Cashmere sweater? Dog bed. Newspaper? Tug-of-war toy.

Sometimes dogs who have lived for a long time under "traditional" rules have a hard time unlearning the conditioning they received as puppies. They've been brainwashed into believing that dogs are only allowed to handle things that stay on the ground, while everything else in the house belongs to humans. You can undo this by putting his toys on tables and chairs, within his reach but not on the floor, and by giving him your old possessions to play with. He won't know the difference between old socks and new socks, so he'll quickly graduate to chewing up the good ones.

The Well-Rounded VBD

Now that you've got basic skills instilled, you're well on your way to having a top-notch VBD. Even though you're probably already unbearably proud (of yourself as well as your precious pup), there's more. What's next? Advanced VBD behavior!

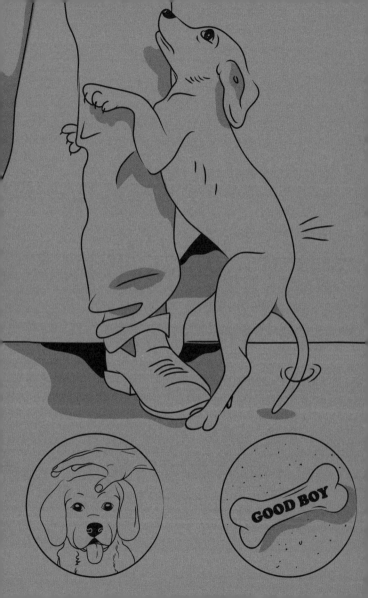

GOOD BOY

ADVANCED VBD SKILLS

8 CROTCH-SNIFFING AND BEYOND

As we explore even more progressive concepts to cultivate in the VBD, it's important to remember the basic tenets of canine behavior modification outlined in chapter 6: reward heavily and often for those very bad behaviors that you'd like your dog to repeat. Sometimes, once the fundamental skills are in place, owners relax on reinforcement. While at this point you already have a competent VBD, if you want to go to the next level, don't allow yourself to slack. With advanced behaviors, life with the VBD just gets more interesting, fun, and all consuming, so why deny yourself this level of development?

In this chapter, you will learn:

- How to encourage your dog to urinate on your guests.

- Why begging really *is* cute after all.

- How to encourage your dog to protect your car.

- A few extremely advanced behaviors for the truly adventurous VBD and her owner.

Crotch-Sniffing, Humping, and Marking Strangers

You've probably noticed that dogs sniff one another's private parts. While this may seem invasive to people, for dogs that's where all the good stuff is—glands and hormones that communicate information such as gender, whether the dog has been spayed or neutered or is pregnant, if the dog is healthy, even what the dog eats. Of course, a dog's nose is many times stronger than a humans, and it's her primary mode of taking in the world. Why wouldn't dogs want to get to know humans in this way? Crotch-sniffing is the canine equivalent of shaking hands and asking, "Have we met?"

When your dog greets a stranger, allow her to explore her sense of smell. Don't accidentally correct her; instead, affectionately repeat the dog's name, smile with embarrassment, and make excuses.

Humping is another dramatic behavior that can best be encouraged by actively following the dominance-permission program detailed in chapter 5 as well as by avoiding any accidental humping aversives. If your dog is a humper, he will likely be humping toy animals, pillows, and other dogs already. It's not a big leap for him to include people. Protest enough to assuage your friends, but not enough to deter your dog.

Marking strangers (peeing on them) is one of the hardest behaviors to encourage in VBDs, only because a successful dog will sadly be rewarded with a swift kick, an aversive substantial enough to forever quell the behavior. Unneutered males excel most at this behavior, which you can foster by allowing your dog to urinate on walks whenever and wherever he pleases. An intact male who is encouraged to mark his territory will often

VBD Hall of Fame: Nuzzle Harassment

In 1997, a class-action lawsuit was filed against a Connecticut judge, alleging that he sexually harassed women and violated their constitutional rights by allowing his golden retriever, Kodak, to "aggressively nuzzle" and "project his snout upward" under their skirts in the courtroom. Fortunately for VBDs everywhere, the district judge who heard the case ruled that the women were "barking up the wrong tree."

mistake a human leg for a post or tree. If you're lucky enough to achieve this behavior, don't try to stop him in the middle of his business. Instead, focus on helping the person to clean up afterward.

Begging for Food

Current trends discourage begging. This recent prejudice in no way detracts from what people have thought for millennia: it's cute, a great way to bond with your dog, and, of course, the very motivation that brought dogs and humans together in the first place (see chapter 4, "What Do They Really Want? Understanding Your VBD's Drives").

Fortunately, begging is one of the easiest behaviors to instill. Don't stop at cute begging, the kind where a little dog sits up and poses on her hind legs. Go to the next level: the demanding beggar.

The desires of the demanding beggar are satisfied almost all the time, unlike the dog who has to sing for her supper. The demanding beggar is a properly cultivated VBD who believes she is dominant. Your food is her food. If your dog even looks at you while you have food in your hand, share it. By feeding your dog bits and pieces of anything you're eating, or by dropping food near the table at dinner, you'll soon have a dog that will not only beg for anything, she'll also push the point.

Counter-Surfing and Foraging

A dog who forages for her food is far more stimulated than one who simply finds it every morning in the food dish. To alleviate boredom and improve overall mental health, zookeepers and biologists provide wild animals in captivity with "food puzzles" to solve before they are rewarded with food. This stimulation and satisfaction of the foraging impulse is so important that the USDA has mandated the use of "foraging or task-oriented feeding methods" in its "Laws, Regulations, and Policies for Environmental Enhancement for Nonhuman Primates." Why deprive our canine friends of the same opportunities?

Teach your dog that rewards come to those who look. Dogs can often unearth long-forgotten morsels of food that we have carelessly left in trash cans, compost buckets, and fast-food containers left on the coffee table. Leave full garbage bags out on the floor. Most likely, your dog will have taken advantage of the foraging opportunity before you can dispose of it.

The easiest place to practice foraging is the kitchen counter. Once your VBD realizes that this locale is a predictable and lucrative resource, your dog will freely graze off your Corian. If you have a small dog, leave a chair she can use as a jumping point, thus encouraging greater exploration of her environment. Be sure to reinforce this behavior by occasionally leaving aromatic foods, such as sliced roast beef, near the edge of the counter.

Encourage your dog to help you clean up by licking the food off dishes that have been loaded into the dishwasher. Not only is this exciting and fun for your dog, it also saves wear and tear on your dishwasher. Simply load the dishes up and leave the door to the dishwasher down. This behavior never fails to impress guests at a dinner party!

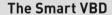

The Smart VBD

Scientists in Germany have proved that dogs know whether we're watching them and are very attuned to our eyes. In the study, if dogs were being watched, they took indirect, deliberately secretive approaches to stealing forbidden food. When researchers appeared to be engrossed in a computer game or had their eyes shut, however, dogs went directly to forbidden food and stole twice as much.

Riding in the Car with Your VBD

Riding in the car with a VBD has the potential to become one of the most exciting parts of your day. Bolstered by the false sense of confidence an elevated auto provides, dogs can be encouraged to become absolute tyrants in the car. Barking, howling, or aggressive behavior toward approaching humans or other dogs will not be uncommon, particularly if you've instilled a strong repertoire of defensive and neurotic behaviors in your dog.

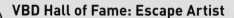

VBD Hall of Fame: Escape Artist

Rosco, an American bulldog living in Virginia Beach, gets the Houdini prize. During a 2006 stay in an animal-control facility, he chewed open the latch to his kennel and climbed over a 7-foot concrete wall topped with barbed wire. When he was caught the next day swimming in a lake some 4 miles away, Rosco turned himself in without incident.

Dogs should never be confined or tied up while in the car. Instead, learn how to drive in ways that accommodate your dog's wanderings, even if that includes stepping on your lap and obscuring your line of vision. Although some people will tell you that dogs shouldn't ride with their heads sticking out of the car windows, your dog's palpable pleasure at doing so will tell you that denying such a fulfilling activity would be nothing short of cruel. In fact, dogs should be encouraged to explore beyond the window—which of course should be fully open.

Encourage your VBD to guard the car aggressively by leaving her alone in the car with the windows cracked open while you go shopping. If you've spent the time to antisocialize your dog, she will most likely be leery of passersby. To develop this quality, start off by parking away from areas with lots of foot traffic so she doesn't become conditioned to people walking by the car. Then, when you later switch to more crowded areas, she will no doubt respond by vigorously protecting her mobile home.

Escaping from the House

Dogs love to explore the outside world. In fact, before our culture became the litigious, keep-to-yourself one we live in today, dogs roamed their neighborhoods freely. That was a golden age for dogs. We can have it again—why hold your VBD hostage to your schedule?

Dogs will naturally wander from home, particularly if there's a good reason. Small dogs find it thrilling to dart out the front door when a delivery or guest arrives. If you chase her, loudly calling her name, it's even more exciting to evade capture. Make sure that you encourage this game of catch-me-if-you-can by accidentally leaving the front door open on occasion.

Your VBD will also enjoy dismantling or circum-venting the barriers between her and the outside world. Encouragement techniques include:

- **Climbing fences.** Wire or chain link is easier for a dog to negotiate than wood or cinder block. If you must install wood, make sure that there are crossbars applied to at convenient intervals to facilitate traction. Or, make your fence low enough for your dog to jump over.

- **Digging under fences and gates.** A nicely aerated section of fresh topsoil will encourage dogs to dig. Avoid wire mesh, gravel, concrete, and rocks under your fences as they can deter your dog from further excavation.

- **Unlatching gates.** A simple latch is easy for many dogs to open, if they can reach it. Make sure to move the latch to waist height if you have a smaller dog. Under no circumstances should you clip the gate with a lock or snap.

> ### Canine Quip
>
> *"If you don't want your dog to have bad breath, do what I do: pour a little Lavoris in the toilet."*
>
> **—Jay Leno**

Identifying Opportunities for Even More Very Bad Behavior

After learning all the techniques in this book, you may feel that your dog could not get any worse. We're happy to tell you that we've just scratched the surface! With your new grasp of the fundamentals, you'll have no trouble introducing the following behaviors to your VBD:

- Ferociously guarding children from their parents

- Eating holes in drywall

- Chewing up door handles

- Herding guests into one room and holding them hostage

- Obsessively fixating on dust particles

- Screaming (half whine, half howl)

- Uprooting the wall-to-wall carpet

- Consuming other household pets

These are all actual, verified problems seen in exceptional VBDs. But if you've plateaued in your VBD development, consider sending your dog to a friend or relative for a few days. A week with a permissive uncle can do wonders for very bad behavior. A small absence can give your dog the time and space she needs to come up with ever more imaginative poor behaviors.

Creativity Above All

As you probably gleaned thus far, ingenuity is tremendously important in maintaining the momentum of your VBD's progress. You've now given your dog the tools and self-reliance she needs to choose her own VBD path, and soon she'll make the worst decisions for herself. But it's not over yet—in the next chapter, you'll learn about the holy grails of very bad behavior: neurosis and aggression.

NEUROTIC AND AGGRESSIVE ANTICS

 9

TRY THESE AT HOME

Thus far we've led you through fairly standard VBD behaviors. Now, in our last instructional section, we're going to share with you secrets of the *ne plus ultra* of the VBD: a dog who is either categorically crazy or aggressively dangerous. Who would want such dogs? Recall the dog-owning types of chapter 2. Generally, owners with their own neurotic tendencies—especially those motivated to own dogs as replacement humans or therapists— cultivate dogs with neuroses. And, as you might guess, owners who are compensating for their own inadequacies prize the violent, aggressive VBD. We do have to warn you that violent VBDs can cause problems. As famed Supreme Court justice Oliver

Wendell Holmes Jr., stated, "The right to swing my fist ends where the other man's nose begins." As all of us know, however, there will always be individuals compensating for their own inadequacies by fostering aggression in their VBDs, and if they choose to do so, they might as well do it right.

In this chapter, we'll show you:

- How to leave the house in a way that maximizes separation anxiety.

- How your VBD can learn new neuroses at doggy day care.

- Why you should immediately caress your dog if he's barking, growling, or snarling.

- Why you should leave your VBD in the front yard.

Separation Anxiety: The Spoils of Codependence

Separation anxiety is the hottest new disorder among canines, and luckily, it's one of the easiest to encourage. No longer can dogs just loll about,

Doggy Dictionary: Bark Mitzvah

In the Jewish tradition, a bark mitzvah welcomes your VBD into adulthood with a gala thirteenth-birthday celebration.

entertaining themselves in the backyard. Instead, the modern dog spends the majority of his time in the house, waiting for you to return, without any stimulation or access to exercise while you are gone. This kind of environment is ripe for developing a good case of separation anxiety.

A dog who feels abandoned is prone to all kinds of poor behavior, including chewing things that smell like you, gnawing on the furniture, urinating inside the house, barking until the neighbors complain, clawing doors, boring holes in the drywall, knocking stuff over, and even launching himself through windows and doors.

If your dog does not exhibit any of these reactions and seems placid around your departures and returns, here are a few easy ways to encourage separation anxiety:

- **Make comings and goings extremely emotional.** Highly charged outpourings are the key to developing a strong anxious response in your absence. When you leave, swoon over your dog, petting and doting on him, telling him you'll be back soon. When you return, make the reunion extremely exciting by ferociously petting your dog and speaking to him in a high-pitched, excited voice, allowing him to jump on you and lick you all over. These episodes create a sharp contrast between your presence and your absence, a critical dynamic to developing the correct pattern of anxiety.

- **Ritualize your exits.** Develop a routine (collect your keys and put on your coat) to cue your dog to your departure. This way he can work up to the maximum anxiety level. Your dog must know you're gone in order to fall to pieces.

- **Leave your dog with nothing to do.** If you provide your VBD with chew toys, bones, or anything else with which he can distract himself, he may not remember to become anxious.

- **Encourage intense bonding with your dog.**
  Make sure your dog plays *the* central role in your
  life. Let him sleep in bed with you, cuddle often,
  and plan your day around his needs. Lavish him
  with affection, treats, and constant attention.
  The goal is to have him believe that without you
  present, his world will fall apart. This does not,
  however, work with boyfriends.

The Obsessive-Compulsive VBD

Dogs that exhibit what some owners might call
"obsessive-compulsive disorder" (OCD) are truly
fascinating to watch. Unfortunately, these traits
are very difficult to cultivate in dogs that don't have
a genetic predisposition for OCD. Indeed, OCD is
thought to result from inbreeding, especially in
German shepherds, rottweilers, dalmatians, and
bulldogs. Canine OCD manifests itself as fixations,
repetitive behaviors that the dog cannot seem to
stop (called stereotypies), and self-mutilation. For
example, some dogs will hunt for lost objects to the
exclusion of all other activities, even eating. Others
incessantly pace, lick themselves until they create
sores, or chase their tails.

OCD behavior is frequently found in dogs with high hunt and prey drives, lots of energy, and very little else to do. These OCD tendencies are, ironically, an excellent quality to have in dogs used for search-and-rescue or drug detection because they are single-minded about the task at hand. Indeed, German shepherds are most often used for police work. If you're lucky enough to have one of these dogs, bore them to tears and then hide their ball.

The Glory of Whining

Whining is a one of the best neurotic behaviors to encourage in the VBD because once the behavior has been instilled, it's almost impossible to stop. Promote whining by crating your dog. When he begins to vocalize, immediately reward him by opening the crate door.

Many dogs will whimper quietly, but your goal is a plaintive wail. To encourage more varied and expressive whining, utilize the principle of the jackpot theory (see chapter 6, "Rewards and Deterrents: Very Bad Behavior Modification"). When your dog gives a particularly mournful cry, reward. Your dog will soon learn that the more heart-wrenching pleas get him out of the crate sooner.

To generalize this behavior to the outside world, teach your VBD that whining will get him what he wants. If he whines at the door, drop everything and take him for a walk. If he whines at the vet, remove him from the exam room and go home. If he whines at the refrigerator, give him a steak.

Effective Reinforcement for Barking and Growling

Barking is a universal dog behavior that every VBD should know. Most dogs naturally bark at strange noises at night or at the sound of the doorbell ringing. If you catch your dog barking, praise him well and encourage it with a lively "Yes, Fido!" Even calling his name out and telling him to be quiet will accomplish your goals.

If you don't have a naturally gifted barker, you can often create one by allowing your dog to hang out with a barker, as barking lends itself well to mimicking. One of the best places to find good barkers is at doggy day care. These facilities usually have many different kinds of dogs, so there's bound to be a good barker among them. Visit the day cares in your area ahead of time to ascertain which is the loudest. Within a few days, your dog will learn to bark confidently, and with any luck he'll transfer that behavior to his home environment.

Rewarding Displays of Aggression

Dogs will naturally display aggression when faced with threats, and barking followed by growling are often precursors to snapping, biting, or fighting. Here are some easy exercises to promote aggressive behavior:

1. **Present your dog with a "threat," such as a strange visitor.** Hopefully, your previous antisocialization has resulted in your dog perceiving anyone outside your home as a potential threat.

2. **Pet your dog.** When your dog reacts aggressively by barking, growling, or snarling, kneel down, pet him calmly, and say, "Easy, easy." This will communicate to your dog that aggression is the correct response.

3. **Remove the threat.** Either wait until the "threat" moves away or drag your barking dog off. This teaches the dog that displays of aggression work. Threats go away.

Cultivating Overprotectiveness

Like humans, dogs display aggression around items that are of value to them; as this is a natural tendency, it will probably rise on its own if you cultivate other territorial behaviors. Not only will your overprotective VBD guard things he should (like your house), he'll guard arbitrary things. A dog protective of what most people would deem inappropriate is a VBD grand slam! Examples of overprotected objects include children, other pets, laundry, Christmas gifts, and even the toilet.

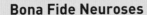

Bona Fide Neuroses

Your VBD has at his disposal a wide variety of specific anxieties and neuroses. While some are genetic in origin, these conditions can all be encouraged by providing your dog with as few social opportunities and as little exercise as possible.

Diagnosis	Description
Acral lick dermatitis	Obsessive licking, usually on paws or legs, that results in skin lesions.
Astraphobia	Fear of thunderstorms.
Coprophagia	Ingesting feces.
Displaced sex drive	Humping invisible mates.
Pica	Ingesting nonfood items, like rocks, drywall, and socks.
Spinning (tail-chasing)	Compulsive spinning in circles, often for hours on end.
Submissive urination	Urination when faced with uncomfortable social contact.

Territorial Aggression: Maximum K-9 Defense at Home

Most dogs will naturally exhibit some territorial aggression if they've lived long enough in one spot. Even dogs who have small territories (for example, chained-up dogs) try to protect their small patch of the universe. Here's how to encourage vicious displays of aggression against potential intruders:

- **Leave your dog in the front yard.** Dogs in front yards are much more likely to become aggressive than their backyard counterparts simply because there is more traffic to defend against.

- **Promote visual contact.** Allow visual contact with potential intruders, but keep your dog behind the fence.

- **Install a large bay window.** If you don't have a front yard, a bay window is a necessity. This will allow your dog to run back and forth in the window, defending your house from passersby. If you have a small dog, a sofa placed under the window will do.

- **Get a second dog.** There is nothing better to encourage aggressive displays than a second dog. Even relatively meek dogs will feed off the self-assurance of another dog and join in when it comes time to protect their territory.

Just Say No

Dogs are right behind people when it comes to the use of psychotropic drugs—antidepressants, antianxiety medications, etc. Since the passing of a 1994 act legalizing the treatment of pets with human drugs not approved for animals ("off-label use"), this anti-VBD medical trend is on the rise.

Drug	Human Ailments Treated	Canine Ailments Treated
Prozac	Depression, OCD, bulimia, panic disorder	Separation anxiety
Valium	Anxiety disorders	Separation anxiety, phobias
Lithium Carbonate	Bipolar disorder	Aggression

Who Needs Prozac?

Veterinarians are prescribing ever-increasing quantities of canine antidepressants and antianxiety medications. Apparently, dog lovers and haters alike want to limit your VBD rights. And that's what we'll address in the final chapter, because no doubt after experiencing this process you'll want to become a VBD advocate.

VBD LOVERS UNITE!

10 CONCLUSION

Congratulations, VBD lover—you've done it! After lots of hard but enjoyable work, you've cultivated your very own VBD. Once you've lived with a VBD for a while, you'll probably start to notice that not everybody appreciates your approach to dog behavior. In fact, there are looming naysayers who seek to curtail your VBD rights. After appreciating the joys of the VBD, you'll want to spread the word and garner support for this complex companion animal.

There are many reasons to agitate for the VBD cause. Enemies of the VBD include landlords, neighbors, passersby, and even other dog owners in venues like dog parks. Your neighbors can get an injunction against your barking VBD or take you to small-claims court and force you to pay damages for their lost sleep or quality of life. There's even a type of lawyer known as a dog-bite attorney! From leash laws and pooper-scooper rules to outlawed breeds and mandatory sterilization, your rights as a dog owner are under constant attack.

United VBD lovers stand, divided they fall, so you'll want to go out into the world and find others who share your special beliefs. Until the movement gathers strength, the best way to find like-minded souls is to patronize places where dogs gather, especially dog parks. At these parks, take the opportunity to observe how others behave with their dogs (since you won't be watching yours, you'll be free to look around). You'll be able to identify other dog owners who don't keep an eye on their dogs, encourage aggression, or repeat ineffectual commands. Approach those people and let them know about your commitment to the VBD. Tell them how well your household runs now that your VBD is the center of the universe. Before you know it, you'll have a support group that could one day become a political action committee!

As a VBD owner and advocate, there's only one more thing to do. Think back to the "Multiple-Dog Households" section of chapter 3. Now that you've accomplished one VBD, don't you think it's time for another?